HEALTH &
WELL-BEING

In the Words of 'Abdu'l-Bahá

BAHÁ'Í
PUBLISHING

WILMETTE, ILLINOIS

Bahá'í Publishing
401 Greenleaf Avenue, Wilmette, Illinois 60091
Copyright © 2021 by the National Spiritual Assembly
of the Bahá'ís of the United States
All rights reserved. Published 2021

Printed in the United States of America on acid-free paper ∞
24   23   22   21   4   3   2   1

ISBN 978-1-61851-200-0

Cover design by Carlos Esparza
Book design by Patrick Falso

Extracts 2, 3, 5–7, 13, 14, 17, 18, 20, 21, 26 are from *Selections from the Writings of 'Abdu'l-Bahá*. Wilmette, IL: Bahá'í Publishing, 2010.

Extracts 9, 19, 22, 25 are from *Some Answered Questions*. Haifa: Bahá'í World Centre, 2014.

Extract 8 is from *'Abdu'l-Bahá in London: Addresses and Notes of Conversations*. London: Bahá'í Publishing Trust, 1982.

Extracts 8, 16, 27, 28 are from *Paris Talks: Addresses Given by 'Abdu'l-Bahá in Paris in 1911*. Wilmette, IL: Bahá'í Publishing, 2011.

Extracts 1, 4, 10, 11, 12, 15, 23, 24 are from *The Promulgation of Universal Peace: Talks Delivered by 'Abdu'l-Bahá during His Visit to the United States and Canada in 1912*. Wilmette, IL: Bahá'í Publishing, 2012.

'Abdu'l-Bahá

November 2021 will mark the hundredth anniversary of the passing of a figure beloved by many. 'Abdu'l-Bahá, meaning *Servant of the Glory,* is the title assumed by Abbás Effendi (1844–1921), the son and appointed successor of Bahá'u'lláh—the Prophet and Founder of the Bahá'í Faith. 'Abdu'l-Bahá shared a lifetime of exile with his Father at the hands of the Persian and Ottoman Empires, and was a prisoner for forty years. Despite the severe hardships that characterized his life, he dedicated his energy to the service of others and radiated joy and selfless contentment at all times. His charitable deeds and undiscriminating love for all are well documented in the accounts of countless souls who crossed his path, and his timeless and deep wisdom is recorded extensively in both his written works and in the transcripts of his many public addresses. He is known by Bahá'ís as the perfect exemplar of the Faith's teachings.

1

Christ was a heavenly Physician. He brought spiritual health and healing into the world. Bahá'u'lláh is, likewise, a divine Physician. He has revealed prescriptions for removing disease from the body politic and has remedied human conditions by spiritual power.

2

There are two ways of healing sickness, material means and spiritual means. The first is by the treatment of physicians; the second consisteth in prayers offered by the spiritual ones to God and in turning to Him. Both means should be used and practiced.

3

Although ill health is one of the unavoidable conditions of man, truly it is hard to bear. The bounty of good health is the greatest of all gifts.

4

. . . some souls are weak; we must endeavor to strengthen them. Some are ignorant, uninformed of the bounties of God; we must strive to make them knowing. Some are ailing; we must seek to restore them to health. Some are immature as children; they must be trained and assisted to attain maturity. We nurse the sick in tenderness and the kindly spirit of love; we do not despise them because they are ill. Therefore, we must exercise extreme patience, sympathy and love toward all mankind, considering no soul as rejected.

5

Illnesses which occur by reason of physical causes should be treated by doctors with medical remedies; those which are due to spiritual causes disappear through spiritual means. Thus an illness caused by affliction, fear, nervous impressions, will be healed more effectively by spiritual rather than by physical treatment. Hence, both kinds of treatment should be followed; they are not contradictory. Therefore thou shouldst also accept physical remedies inasmuch as these too have come from the mercy and favor of God, Who hath revealed and made manifest medical science so that His servants may profit from this kind of treatment also. Thou shouldst give equal attention to spiritual treatments, for they produce marvelous effects.

6

If humankind . . . lived according to a natural, inborn equilibrium, without following wherever their passions led, it is undeniable that diseases would no longer take the ascendant, nor diversify with such intensity.

7

Now, if thou wishest to know the true remedy which will heal man from all sickness and will give him the health of the divine kingdom, know that it is the precepts and teachings of God. Focus thine attention upon them.

8

All true healing comes from God! There are two causes for sickness, one is material, the other spiritual. If the sickness is of the body, a material remedy is needed, if of the soul, a spiritual remedy.

If the heavenly benediction be upon us while we are being healed then only can we be made whole, for medicine is but the outward and visible means through which we obtain the heavenly healing. Unless the spirit be healed, the cure of the body is worth nothing. All is in the hands of God, and without Him there can be no health in us!

9

As to physical agents, which are the primary cause of illness, their effect is due to the following: The human body is composed of numerous elements according to a particular state of equilibrium. So long as this equilibrium is maintained, man is preserved from sickness, but should this fundamental balance, which is the central requirement of a sound constitution, be upset, the constitution will be disrupted and illness will supervene.

10

If any trouble or vicissitude comes into your lives, if your heart is depressed on account of health, livelihood or vocation, let not these things affect you. They should not cause unhappiness, for Bahá'u'lláh has brought you divine happiness. He has prepared heavenly food for you; He has destined eternal bounty for you; He has bestowed everlasting glory upon you. Therefore, these glad tidings should cause you to soar in the atmosphere of joy forever and ever. Render continual thanks unto God so that the confirmations of God may encircle you all.

11

Happiness is a great healer to those who are ill.

12

Spirit has influence; prayer has spiritual effect. Therefore, we pray, "O God! Heal this sick one!" Perchance God will answer. Does it matter who prays? God will answer the prayer of every servant if that prayer is urgent. . . .

But we ask for things which the divine wisdom does not desire for us, and there is no answer to our prayer. His wisdom does not sanction what we wish.

13

When giving medical treatment turn to the Blessed Beauty, then follow the dictates of thy heart. Remedy the sick by means of heavenly joy and spiritual exultation, cure the sorely afflicted by imparting to them blissful glad tidings and heal the wounded through His resplendent bestowals. When at the bedside of a patient, cheer and gladden his heart and enrapture his spirit through celestial power. Indeed, such a heavenly breath quickeneth every moldering bone and reviveth the spirit of every sick and ailing one.

14

O ye, God's loved ones! Experience hath shown how greatly the renouncing of smoking, of intoxicating drink, and of opium, conduceth to health and vigor, to the expansion and keenness of the mind and to bodily strength.

15

Bahá'u'lláh is the real Physician. He has diagnosed human conditions and indicated the necessary treatment. The essential principles of His healing remedies are the knowledge and love of God, severance from all else save God, turning our faces in sincerity toward the Kingdom of God, implicit faith, firmness and fidelity, loving-kindness toward all creatures and the acquisition of the divine virtues indicated for the human world. These are the fundamental principles of progress, civilization, international peace and the unity of mankind. These are the essentials of Bahá'u'lláh's teachings, the secret of everlasting health, the remedy and healing for man.

It is my hope that you may assist in healing the sick body of the world through these teachings so that eternal radiance may illumine all the nations of mankind.

16

How often do we see a man, poor, sick, miserably clad, and with no means of support, yet spiritually strong. Whatever his body has to suffer, his spirit is free and well! Again, how often do we see a rich man, physically strong and healthy, but with a soul sick unto death.

17

It is incumbent upon everyone to seek medical treatment and to follow the doctor's instructions, for this is in compliance with the divine ordinance, but, in reality, He Who giveth healing is God.

18

O handmaid of God! The prayers which were revealed to ask for healing apply both to physical and spiritual healing. Recite them, then, to heal both the soul and the body. If healing is right for the patient, it will certainly be granted; but for some ailing persons, healing would only be the cause of other ills, and therefore wisdom doth not permit an affirmative answer to the prayer.

19

Man's body may become weak or robust, sick or healthy, tired or rested; it may suffer the loss of a hand or leg; it may decline in material powers; it may become blind, deaf, dumb, or paralysed—in short, it may become gravely impaired. And yet, despite this, the spirit maintains its original condition and spiritual perceptions, suffering no impairment or disruption.

20

O ye lovers of God! The world is even as a human being who is diseased and impotent, whose eyes can see no longer, whose ears have gone deaf, all of whose powers are corroded and used up. Wherefore must the friends of God be competent physicians who, following the holy Teachings, will nurse this patient back to health. Perhaps, God willing, the world will mend, and become permanently whole, and its exhausted faculties will be restored, and its person will take on such vigor, freshness and verdancy that it will shine out with comeliness and grace.

21

Haste thou to life before death cometh; haste thou to the spring season before autumn draweth in; and before illness striketh, haste thou to healing—that thou mayest become a physician of the spirit who, with the breaths of the Holy Spirit, healeth all manner of sickness in this famed and glorious age.

22

. . . the human spirit is always in one condition. It neither falls ill with the illness of the body nor is made healthy by the latter's health; it does not become weak or incapacitated, wretched or downtrodden, diminished or lessened—that is, it suffers no harm or ill effect on account of the infirmities of the body, even if the body were to waste away, or if the hands, feet, and tongue were to be cut off, or if the powers of sight and hearing were to be disrupted. It is therefore evident and established that the spirit is different from the body and that its immortality is not conditioned upon the latter's, but that the spirit rules supreme in the world of the body, and that its power and influence are as plain and visible as the bounty of the sun in a mirror. But when the mirror is covered with dust or broken, it will be deprived of the rays of the sun.

23

The world of humanity may be likened to the individual man himself; it has its illness and ailments. A patient must be diagnosed by a skillful physician. The Prophets of God are the real Physicians. In whatever age or time They appear They prescribe for human conditions. They know the sicknesses; They discover the hidden sources of disease and indicate the necessary remedy. Whosoever is healed by that remedy finds eternal health.

24

Science cannot cure the illness of the body politic. Science cannot create amity and fellowship in human hearts. Neither can patriotism nor racial allegiance effect a remedy. It must be accomplished solely through the divine bounties and spiritual bestowals which have descended from God in this day for that purpose. This is an exigency of the times, and the divine remedy has been provided. The spiritual teachings of the religion of God can alone create this love, unity and accord in human hearts.

25

. . . the parts and members of the human body mutually influence one another. For instance, the eye sees and the heart is affected. The ear hears and the spirit is influenced. The heart finds peace, the thoughts expand, and all the members of the body experience a state of well-being. What a connection and relationship this is!

26

Matters related to man's spirit have a great effect on his bodily condition. For instance, thou shouldst impart gladness to thy patient, give him comfort and joy, and bring him to ecstasy and exultation. How often hath it occurred that this hath caused early recovery. Therefore, treat thou the sick with both powers. Spiritual feelings have a surprising effect. . . .

27

Oh! put your faith in the Almighty, for He faileth not and His goodness endureth forever! His Sun giveth Light continually, and the Clouds of His Mercy are full of the Waters of Compassion with which He waters the hearts of all who trust in Him. His refreshing Breeze ever carries healing in its wings to the parched souls of men!

28

If we are sick and in distress let us implore God's healing, and He will answer our prayer.

When our thoughts are filled with the bitterness of this world, let us turn our eyes to the sweetness of God's compassion and He will send us heavenly calm! If we are imprisoned in the material world, our spirit can soar into the Heavens and we shall be free indeed!